High Calling
High Anxiety

O. S. HAWKINS

ISBN: 0-9671584-6-X

Dewey Decimal Classification: 227.91, dc 21

Subject Heading: BIBLE. N. T. JAMES\\CLERGY — JOB
STRESS\\ANXIETY — RELIGIOUS ASPECTS

Printed in the United States of America

Unless otherwise noted, Scripture quotations are the Holy Bible,
New King James version or the New International version.

ANNUITY BOARD
OF THE SOUTHERN
BAPTIST CONVENTION

Other books by O.S. Hawkins

When Revival Comes

After Revival Comes

Clues to a Successful Life

Where Angels Fear to Tread

Tracing the Rainbow Through the Rain

Unmasked: Recognizing and Dealing with Imposters in the Church

Revive Us Again

Jonah: Meeting the God of the Second Chance

Getting Down to Brass Tacks: Advice from James for Real World Christians

In Sheep's Clothing

Tearing Down Walls and Building Bridges

Moral Earthquakes and Secret Faults

Rebuilding: It's Never too Late for a New Beginning

Money Talks: But What Is It Really Saying?

Shields of Brass or Shields of Gold? Re-establishing a Standard of Excellence in the Church of the Lord Jesus Christ

Good News for Great Days

Drawing the Net

Culture Shock

Dedication

Jack Pogue

Like thousands of Christian laymen he finds his joy in encouraging and in serving those who are called to be God's ministers in the church. It was Jack's high calling to tenderly meet the constant needs of Dr. W.A. Criswell, especially during the last years of his good and godly life. Like Barnabas, Jack is a true "son of encouragement." And, also like Barnabas, he uses his resources to advance Kingdom business. Thanks to this dedicated layman and the Criswell Legacy which he founded, we now have wacriswell.com *where, free of any charge, Bible students all over the world now have access to almost 2,000 of Dr. Criswell's sermons both in print and on video.*

Thank you, Jack. "Your love has given us great hope and encouragement because you, brother, have refreshed the hearts of the saints" (Philemon 7).

Table of contents

Appendices

Foreword

High Calling — High Anxiety

Genesis 6:3 says man should live 120 years. I am convinced that the reason we do not live that long is not because of a "design deficiency," but the way we treat our bodies. It has been said that "when a man dies, he dies not so much of the disease he has, he dies of his entire life."

Without question, stress and anxiety adversely affect and shorten our lives, but it is not stress that kills, it is the way it is handled. The famous stress expert Hans Selye once said, "Stress is the spice of life. What would life be like if there were no runs, no hits, and no errors?" The best way to control stress physiologically is to exercise, particularly at the end of a stressful day prior to the evening meal. I know, since that is what I have been doing successfully for over 40 years to control both my weight and the stress in my life.

A few years ago I conducted a small study comparing full-time ministers with physicians who came to the

Cooper Clinic for examinations. They were matched only according to their age (mid 40s), and in every test parameter the physicians out-performed the pastors, even though the physicians certainly could not be classified as being in good condition.

I presented this data to a large group of pastors attending the Pastors Conference being held in conjunction with the 1992 Southern Baptist Convention in Indianapolis, Indiana. After the presentation, one of the attendees told me that he enjoyed my remarks, but the man sitting next to him obviously did not. He said that throughout the presentation the man "kept fidgeting and shifting about in his chair, obviously disturbed with what I was saying." At the conclusion of my remarks, the man leaned over to him and said, "That was terrible! This shouldn't be featured at a pastor's conference. We should be concentrating on spiritual issues, not something affecting the flesh!" The attendee looked at the man and noted that he must have weighed at least 300 pounds.

For over 30 years, I have had the privilege of working with men and women who are involved full-time in the ministry. I believe it is one of my "callings" to help these people achieve optimum health and fitness. I know the stress and anxiety under which they live, but I have also noticed that many try to control their stress by increasing the consumption of food. The banquet circuit does not help this situation. Remember, too, "the most common manifestation of stress is obesity, and stressed spelled backwards is desserts!" Obesity is associated with a myriad of medical problems, including osteoarthritis particularly affecting the knees, hypertension, heart disease and diabetes. There is no way that you can "glorify God to the highest" if you are constantly troubled with inactivity- and obesity-related medical problems.

I am convinced that at age 72 I would be unable to work in a highly demanding position, spend long hours at the office six days a week, or travel the world on speaking and consulting engagements if I had not practiced the principles of preventive medicine that Dr. Hawkins describes so eloquently in this book — and I have not missed a day from work due to illness since 1956 when I had an appendectomy.

I strongly agree with the guidelines and recommendations in *High Calling — High Anxiety*, and hope and pray that all those who read this book will benefit to the extent that they will be able to serve Him better!

Kenneth H. Cooper, M.D., M.P.H.
Chairman & Chief Executive Officer
The Cooper Aerobics Center

Introduction

Stress! Perhaps no other word is used as much to describe the culprit, the scapegoat, the excuse of modern man. Most of the problems in our homes and in our health seem to relate to the stress factor. Webster defines stress as "pressure, intense strain; to bind tight, to subject oneself to external forces." A lot of people reading these words are saying to themselves right now, "You are telling Noah about a flood!"

There is high anxiety in the high calling of ministry today. The pressures of the pastorate are especially intense breeding grounds for stress. Stress has been linked to such illnesses as high blood pressure, heart attacks, depression, immune system deficiencies, asthma, gastric disorders, and even cancer. Is it any wonder that the top two prescriptions prescribed to Southern Baptists ministers this past year were both related to stress problems? There is high anxiety in our high calling.

The moment we hear the word, "stress," some of us tighten up. We clench our fists as if stress was our foe. Yet, it can be our friend! In fact, Dr. Kenneth H. Cooper addressed this subject in his book *Can Stress Heal?* The subtitle tells the story, "Converting a major health hazard into a surprising health benefit." When we learn to see stress as a warning signal and deal with it, it can become one of life's greatest assets. It is often God's way of telling us that life is out of balance. Stress does not have to be our foe. It can become our friend. Learning to live with and deal with the high anxiety that comes with our high calling can result in a longer, healthier, and happier life, as well as a more productive life.

Those called to ministry have never been faced with greater issues that lend themselves to stress than those of the 21st century. Many of our lives are overloaded and few of us have what Dr. Richard Swenson calls "margin" left in our lives. We rush to work, rush to our children's activities, rush here and rush there. We take our briefcases home from the office and work an hour or two before going to bed. Then we get up in the morning and fight the irritations associated with traffic and, in more cases than we would like to admit, the personal relationships of irritable people. Stress has become an inevitable part of our daily lives.

I remember well the first time I ever saw a video game when they were being introduced to American culture back in the 1980s. My family and I used to eat dinner at a little

Italian takeout restaurant and they had installed a Pac-Man video game. If you recall, the Pac-Man would run around the video screen eating up all the other dots. Life has become like that Pac-Man game for many of us. It has become so packed and busy that it eats up our entire margin.

One of the things that makes life more difficult for those of us in ministry is the fishbowl effect. That is, in ministry many of us are forced to live our lives in full view and scrutiny of many of those around us. We are expected to be almost superhuman in many ways. We read about our forefathers, those men and women who crossed the oceans and braved bitter winters in the new world. We read how they fought off Indian raids and endured all sorts of calamities. We hear about those in the 19th century who piled their kids into covered wagons and headed out toward the western frontier, out into the unknown. We think about those who have gone before us in the pre-ceding decades who lived through the ordeals of World War I and World War II, Korea, Vietnam, and dozens of other wars and skirmishes. We're prone to think that life is so much easier for us. Yet, it is not!

Everyone is under stress today. Children are under stress living in disintegrating homes, millions of whom have become the product of massive divorces. Teenagers are under stress today, many of them are afraid to go into their public school classrooms. Young adults are under stress, many of whom have graduate degrees but are finding no places to work. Parents are under stress wondering how they are going to educate their children as they go through mid-life crises themselves. Senior adults are under stress. Many of them are spending their life savings on their children and their children's children while all the while hoping against catastrophic illness themselves. This is the world we are called to impact for Christ. And in the midst of it all perhaps no one is under more stress than those who are called to ministry. Terminations of Baptist ministers are at an all time high. Many of our ministers have rising indebtedness while they seek to keep their head above water in a downsized economy. Medical costs are raging out of control on a national level. Pastors are preaching to an aging population in churches that have already lost a couple of generations to a secular culture. Rampant divorce and the disintegration of the family is all around us. Like Pac-Man the stress of life eats away at those of us in ministry. There seems to be little time alone to charge our batteries and many of us are running down. Yes, there is high anxiety in the high calling of ministry today.

We might not know the stress of crossing oceans in wooden boats nor crossing mountains in covered wagons, but those who lived just a decade before us did not experience the increasing stress and pressures under which we now live. There is a skyrocketing pattern of exponential change in practically every area of life. We're all faced with our own limits. There are limits to our time, our energy, our health, our finances. Many are perilously close to burnout. And all the while, we hope beyond hope that things will level out and slow down as they continue to climb higher and get faster.

We are faced with an important question. How do we deal with stress? God knows more about us than we know about ourselves. He gave us the first 12 verses of the Epistle of James to address this very issue.

The letter of James, written sometime between 48 and 50 A.D., was one of the earliest books of the New Testament. It was written by James, the half-brother of our Lord. Our Lord's earthly parents had other children (Matt. 13:15–56). James was one of these in the family of Christ who was the product of the love of Joseph and Mary. During our Lord's earthly ministry James did not believe in him (John 7:1–5). However, we do know that some time after the resurrection of the Lord, Jesus appeared to his brother and James became a believer (I Cor. 15:7).

James grew in the faith of the Lord Jesus Christ and eventually became the undisputed leader of the Jerusalem church and was the moderator of the great Jerusalem council. The Apostle Paul referred to James as "a pillar" of the church (Gal. 2:9). James was undoubtedly a great man of prayer for tradition recalls that his nickname was "camel knees." This was because of the calluses that evidently appeared on his knees from hours of daily prayer.

One might expect a man of this stature to begin his letter by referring to himself as the leader of the church at Jerusalem or even the half-brother of the Lord Jesus. However, this is not the way the book begins. He begins by addressing himself as "a bond servant." This described the one who is so motivated by love that he can never say no to his master. He takes his place of humble service. Talk about a stress buster. The bond servant never worried about what he would eat or wear. All of that was his master's concern. James saw himself as one who had been bought with a price and who was under the control and care of his master.

It is of utmost importance to note to whom James addressed his letter. It was to the twelve tribes which are scattered abroad (James 1:1). He was writing to these early Christians who were, in his words, "scattered abroad." The Greek word is *diaspora*. We get our word "disperse or dispersion" from this Greek word. The Greek word picture is one who is scattering the seeds. It means to scatter, to spread around. After the martyrdom of Stephen in Acts 8, the Christians in Jerusalem were scattered throughout the Roman world. Persecution broke out against the church in Jerusalem and the Bible informs us that "all except the apostles were scattered throughout the world" (Acts 8:1).

As we look at this dispersion today we readily see that God permitted this test on the Jerusalem church for a purpose. Had they not been scattered throughout the world, the people might well have stayed in Jerusalem and no growth would have occurred throughout the world and the Gospel would not have spread. As it was, the result of this *diaspora* was that in one generation the Gospel spread all through the known world to the very bounds of Rome itself.

James was writing this letter to those Christian Jews who were scattered outside of Palestine. He was writing to those who had been dispersed. He was writing to those who had to leave their homes and their jobs and their properties. However, this is not just a letter to Christian Jews outside of Palestine in the 1st century world. There is a real sense in which all Christians are in the *diaspora*. We are living in exile from our eternal, heavenly home. Thus, this letter is a letter from God to each of us. Behind the hand of James is the hand of God Himself penning these words for "holy men of God spoke as they were moved by the Holy Spirit" (II Pet. 1:21).

James is writing to a people of God who are facing all kinds of "trials." He was teaching them, and us, how to deal with stress and pressure that comes to life. Long before all the books on stress that we find on the bookshelves today were written, James addressed the issue here in this book of all books. He is writing to those who are up against it. He's writing to those who are under tremendous stress. And, at the same time, he is writing to those who are wrestling with how to live out what they believe. Consequently, James is extremely practical and at times he is even a bit polemic in his encouragement for each of us to find margin in life.

As I type these words I try to think about the people who initially were reading this letter. There were women who were at their wit's end. They had been uprooted from their homes, their "nests." They found themselves struggling to keep the home together even though they were multitudes of miles away. He was writing to children who were trying to deal with new surroundings and uncertain futures, living now in a completely different culture. He was writing to men who had lost their jobs and everything they had spent their lives building. He was writing to men and women who were literally hanging by a thread and who were under tremendous pressure and great stress. It is as though these words were directly written to those in ministry today who are experiencing high anxiety in their high calling.

One of the great secrets of life is the ability to react properly under stress and pressure. As the verses of James unfold before us in the pages which follow, we shall see that James is addressing the issues which were not simply applicable to a 1st century world but just as valid for a 21st century world. The Epistle of James is not so much a work on theological truth as it is on how to live the Christ life in a pressure packed world. We will find these initial verses to be extremely practical in nature. And, we will hopefully find a word from God for each of our own hearts and lives.

James reveals five fascinating facts about stress. When each of these is truly applied to our lives we can be on the way to transforming stress from our foe to our friend. James begins by informing us that stress is predictable. The fact is, it is not going away. Stress happens. He also reveals that stress is problematic. If we do not learn to deal with it, it can be detrimental and even destructive to our health, our homes, our happiness, and our hopes. Third, he reveals that stress is paradoxical. He says to count it all joy when you fall into various trials (James 1:2). Now, that is a paradoxical thought if ever there was one! James also reveals that stress is purposeful. God sometimes puts us through the furnace of stress so we can come out as gold with a greater purpose than we've ever known before. Finally, James reveals that stress is profitable. It, like so many other things in the Christian life, can eventually work out for our good and His glory.

Yes, there is high anxiety in the high calling of ministry today. Never before have pastors and church workers lived under such tremendous stress. It is the author's prayer and fervent hope that these pages will serve as a launching pad for ministers everywhere to begin to take serious responsibility for their own spiritual, emotional, and physical wellness thus allowing God to help them turn their stress from their foe to their friend.

Chapter 1

Stress is predictable

(James 1:1–2)

James says you are to count it all joy when you fall into various trials (James 1:2). Note carefully that he does not say "if" we fall into various trials. He says "when." The point is — stress is predictable — inevitable, inescapable, unavoidable. We all have it. Some of us have learned to deal with it and some of us haven't. We live in a pressure packed society and stress is predicable. Stress happens to all of us! Often, well meaning friends encourage us to "avoid stress." This is impossible. Stress is predictable. It happens.

We can read the Bible from cover to cover but nowhere will we find a promise that spirit-filled Christians will be immune to sickness and stress, trials and tribulations.

Some people say that if we're living the Spirit-filled life, we have smooth sailing on the sea of God's will. Jesus warned, "In the world you will have tribulation; but be of good cheer, I have overcome the world" (John 16:33).

What do we mean when we speak of stress? The word has become somewhat commonplace in our modern vernacular. How many times have we heard a student exclaim, "I'm stressed out!" Hans Selye, the noted medical doctor from the University of Prague, devoted his life to the development of the first systematic theory of stress. He defines stress as, "essentially the rate of wear and tear on the body." He also acknowledges that "the goal is certainly not to avoid stress. Stress is a part of life."[1] Many of those who have heeded the high calling of ministerial service are overwhelmed by the mounting pressures around them. Pastors today have more occasions for stress than in any generation. There are stress factors at work. There are projects and deadlines and e-mails and cell phones and often unattainable expectations. And for the pastor there are always those three messages needing to be prepared to deliver weekly to the church. Only a pastor can know the constant pressure of this continual assignment. Today's pastor also has increasing pressure with home life. There

[1] *Stress Management for Ministers*, Charles Rassieur; Westminster Press, Philadelphia, Pa.; 1982

is the necessity of giving priority to time with our wives, our children, our parents, our relatives. We need to attend our children's sports activities and school plays, help with homework and a myriad of other activities that only a parent can fulfill.

Not only is there increasing stress in the office and in the home, but also in the personal arena. Terminations of pastors are at an all-time high. A pastor today is under constant pressure to be as articulate and dynamic as a television preacher, and all the while to be servant-hearted and in line with the deacons. The pastor also finds stress in his own personal growth both physically (his health and exercise) and spiritually (his personal devotion and prayer life). One might assume that pastors of larger churches are prone to more stressful circumstances and situations. I am convinced that it is just the opposite. The smaller church pastor has more demands. He has similar demands in sermon preparation but is unable to delegate many of the pastoral and administrative duties and thus is expected to be all things to all people in the church. This brings added stress to the pastor's life. There is high anxiety in our high calling today. Stress is predictable. It is not "if" it comes, but as James says, "when" it comes.

Why is pastoral ministry so stressful today? The unreal expectations placed on many pastors creates in them a workaholic mentality. There is also that tangible/intangible of the conflict that comes from being a leader and a servant at the same time. One trap many pastors fall into is the fact that their self-esteem or self-image is often wrapped up in what they are able to accomplish. Often the inability to produce what one might call a "win-win conflict resolution" makes managing people and leading people increasingly difficult. Because of the nature of the pastorate, many of God's servants are less likely to have a close friend than any other person in the church or the community. Administration overload is rampant in most churches. And all the while the pastor is seen as the rescuer of everyone's problems and the caregiver to everyone's needs. Most pastors I know are overwhelmed with teaching and preaching deadlines and are surrounded by people with whom it is very difficult to work. The pastor is on call 24 hours a day, and seven days a week. No wonder stress is predictable.

There is no other profession where one has to change gears as often as in the pastorate. After a quarter of a century of pastoring churches myself, I can remember more than one day when in the morning I would share in the joy of the birth of a brand-new baby at the hospital with one of our couples, go from there to be with a family that was involved in a tragedy or an automobile accident or attempted suicide or the like, follow this with a funeral of a great saint of God in the afternoon, and eventually end the day with the joyous experience of a wedding in the evening. Stress is a fact of life and it has never been as big an issue for pastors as it is today.

Yes, stress is predictable. It should be noted that some stress can be good for us because it takes us to another level in meeting the challenges of ministry. There is a sense in which we need a degree of stress to motivate us. But too much stress can be detrimental to us not only physically but mentally and spiritually as well. Stress has physical implications. When we are faced with a stressful situation, our body mechanism goes into action and begins to pump adrenaline into our bloodstream. This additional infusion of adrenaline prepares us to either fight or flee. If we do neither, it remains in our system until our body slowly breaks it down and absorbs it. Therefore, high stress levels over long periods of time can cause serious health problems such as high blood pressure, arthritis, diabetes, heart disease, ulcers, chronic backaches and headaches and other unhealthy conditions.

Stress also has mental implications for those in ministry. Depression is real and rampant in the lives of many who serve in ministry today. Stress can also result in spiritual implications. If we are not careful, the pressures can lead us, like Elijah, to run away from God's calling and find our own juniper tree where we sit in defeat and self-pity.

Although stress is predictable, it does not have to be our foe. It can be our friend. In order for this to happen, we must rise to the physical challenges it brings. God never called you to work harder than He worked Himself in the creation event. He took a day off. Many in ministry have forgotten that their body is "the temple of the Holy Spirit." Many of the physical problems that result from stress are related to poor diet, poor exercise habits, and the inability to rest the body. We must also rise to the mental challenges. Isaiah put it like this, "You will keep him in perfect peace, whose mind is stayed on you because he trusts in you" (Is. 26:3). We must also meet the challenges not only of physical rest and mental rest but of spiritual rest also. Jesus said, "Come unto me…and I will give you rest" (Matt. 11:28). Paul had his own prescription for stress. He put it this way, "Do not be anxious about anything, but in everything, by prayer and petition with thanksgiving, present your request to God. And the peace of God, which transcends all understanding, will guard your hearts and minds in Christ Jesus." (Phil. 4:6).

One bi-vocational pastor of a small church pointed out that fatigue seemed to be his biggest stress trigger. "Working a full-time job in addition to all of the activities involved in pastoring a church can lead to a stressful life style," he said. "It is important to remember to take time to relax. Fatigue and frustration can quickly lead to feelings of stress. Throughout the Gospels we see Jesus taking time to be alone, away from everything including His disciples. That is a good principle to follow. I make an effort to plan personal time away from my ministry each week," he explained.

Some people never deal with stress because of the erroneous idea that it will go away. In fact, many who have been admonished to avoid stress have simply had more stress heaped upon them — the stress of not knowing how to cope. Yes, stress is inevitable. It is a question of "when" not "if."

James said that we should consider it joy when we face various "trials." "Trials" is a translation of the Greek word *peirasmos*. *Peirasmos* can mean either "trials" or "temptations." We must note the context. Sometimes James used *peirasmos* to describe outward trials that are designed to teach Christians to stand firm. In other places, he uses the same word to describe inward temptations to cause the Christian to stumble. In verse 2, James used it to mean an outward trial or test.

Not one of us is immune to outward trials that create stress. Interestingly, we never grow out of the possibility of confronting trials. When we study the lives of men and women in the Bible, we find that some of their greatest trials came way down the road of their personal spiritual pilgrimage, not at the beginning of their walk with God.

Consider Moses for example. After seeing the hand of God in so many wonderful ways — the parting of the Red Sea, the cloud by day and the pillar of fire by night, the manifestations of manna every morning — the complaints of the children of Israel tried his patience. He struck the rock instead of speaking to it, perverting the type of Christ. Think of David — the shepherd, psalmist, king, the "man after God's own heart." His greatest trials came after he was on the throne of Israel. And what about Simon Peter, the big fisherman? He had proven his courage so many times before, but when confronted on the last evening of Christ's earthly life, he cowered by the fire outside the house of the High Priest.

No matter who we are or how long we have walked the journey of the Christian life, we will face stress. The sooner we realize that fact, the more quickly we will be able to deal with it. The tragedy of today's tranquilizer mentality is that it simply postpones the day when we eventually will have to face the foe.

James said we should consider it pure joy when we "fall into" trials of many kinds. The word translated here is the Greek word, *peripiptô*. Found only three times in the entire New Testament, *peripiptô* is the word Jesus used to describe the man on the Jericho road. He said, "A certain man went down from Jerusalem to Jericho, and fell among thieves" (Luke 10:30). Here was a guy who rounded a corner and suddenly — WHAM! He was confronted and surrounded by unexpected trouble. There was no warning, no time to run away. Trouble fell upon him. James 1:2 uses the same word to describe how we are sometimes confronted with stressful trials. We sail through life, go around the bend, and WHAM! We "fall into various trials." Stress is indeed predictable.

How many times have we been on this road? Everything seems to be going well and then we get the doctor's report...or the pink slip comes unexpectedly...or death knocks on a loved one's door...or the roof springs a leak...or additional income tax is due...or the new insurance premium has risen astronomically.

How should we react? We should begin by realizing that stress is predictable. Not one of us is immune to it, and not one of us can escape it. God is always testing us to make us stronger. Ask Abraham. God instructed him to sacrifice his only son, Isaac. Ask Joseph, who was thrown into an Egyptian dungeon on a trumped up charge.

Some present-day prophets are promoting a theology that is foreign to the Bible. There are always those preachers around who tell their followers that the cause of sickness or difficulty is sin in their lives or a lack of faith on their part. Many gullible and immature Christians fall victim to this false teaching. Then, when stressful trials come to them, they lose the faith that they thought they had.

All the New Testament writers remind us that trials will come. Peter put it like this, "In this you greatly rejoice, though now for a little while, if need be, you have been grieved by various trials, that the genuineness of your faith, being much more precious than gold that perishes, though it is tested by fire, may be found to the praise, honor, and glory at the revelation of Jesus Christ" (I Pet. 1:6–7).

Paul certainly experienced trials. He knew that stress was predictable. Hear him as he says, "I served the Lord with all humility, with many tears and trials which happened to me by the plotting of the Jews" (Acts 20:19). Even our Lord was not immune to the stressful trials of life. Hear Him in the upper room saying to His disciples, "You are those who have continued with me in my trials" (Luke 22:28).

If anyone ever had the right to be overcome with high anxiety in His high calling it was the Lord Jesus Christ Himself. Talk about stressful circumstances and situations. He was constantly surrounded by the press of the crowds. Wherever

He went, the crowds were pulling on Him and demanding His time and presence. These stressful circumstances and situations were a constant drain upon Him. Whenever Jesus healed someone it took away from His reserves and added to His fatigue. In Luke 8:46 when a woman with a certain disease touched Him, He said, "Somebody touched me; I know that power has gone out from Me." Jesus had no home, no place to lay his head. There was no place to go into His own room and close the door and shut the people out. Add to this the fact that the Pharisees and Sadducees were constantly picking at Him and constantly seeking ways to catch Him in a fault so that they could be done with Him. And, if that were not enough, His own disciples were competing for His attention and arguing among themselves about who of them was the greatest. This is not to mention that our Lord was faced with the stress of the ever-present shadow of His ultimate destiny, the cross and the crucifixion.

Jesus knew better than anyone that stress is predictable. And yet, He almost never appears to be "stressed out." We never find Him wringing His hands and worrying anxiously. He was faced with so many of the same pressures His under-shepherds are faced with today.

How did our Lord deal with the stressful situations that came His way? As we read the Gospels we find Him continually "getting away" for a while. Sometimes we find

Him up on a mountain alone. Other times we find Him in other places going off by Himself to rest and pray, to just be alone. If our Lord needed that, how much more do we need rest and prayer? Many of us have heard of Dr. Hebert Benson's study at the Harvard Medical School on the importance of prayer as it relates to reducing the impact of stress hormones in a person's body. He said, "Repetitive prayer slows a person's heart and breathing rates. It lowers blood pressure and even slows brain waves, all without drugs or surgery." A recent article in *Parade* magazine reported on new research exploring the connection between prayer and how the body heals itself. Johns Hopkins University, with funding from the National Institute of Health, is studying the effects of petitionary prayer on breast cancer patients; while neuroscientists at the University of Pennsylvania are documenting the changes in brain scans of praying nuns. At Baptist Memorial Hospital in Memphis, patients are offered "prayer intervention" before and after bypass surgery. Studies at Dartmouth Medical Center, the University of Miami, Duke University and at several other medical centers all show that individuals who pray and attend religious services regularly have higher survival rates and recover more quickly from depression, alcoholism, hip surgery, drug addiction, stroke, rheumatoid arthritis, heart attacks and bypass surgery. Dr.

Harold Koenig, director of Duke University's Center for the Study of Religion/Spirituality and Health says that prayer "boosts morale, lowers agitation, loneliness and life dissatisfaction and enhances the ability to cope in men, women, the elderly, the young, the healthy and the sick." Time alone with God in prayer and thanksgiving is not only beneficial spiritually, but physically as well. Our Lord kept His priorities in order. He knew that stress was predictable.

As followers of Christ, we face two basic trials: trials of correction and trials of perfection. When we're out of the will of God, He often allows trials to come our way in order to correct our paths. Ask Jonah, the runaway prophet. Trials of perfection, on the other hand, come to us when we're in the will of God, being where God told us to be and doing what God told us to do. Ask the disciples who climbed into the boat at Jesus' command and found them-selves in the midst of a tremendous storm. A true test of our Christian character just may be how we respond when we lose our blessings.

Yes, we will be tested as believers. Paul said that these stressful trials and temptations were "common to man" (I Cor. 10:13). But it is not nearly as essential for us to explain life's trials theologically and philosophically as it is for us to meet them head on and deal with them. Once we realize that stress is predictable, we can move on and learn how to deal with it. High anxiety in our high calling is predictable. It is "when" not "if". Stress happens to all of us. It is predictable.

Chapter 2

Stress is problematic

(James 1:2)

Just because trials — and the stress they produce — are predictable does not mean that we should treat them lightly or avoid facing them. Stress can be problematic. World renowned health and fitness specialist, Dr. Kenneth H. Cooper says, "Make no mistake: stress is your deadly enemy, which you must learn to combat with all the resources at your disposal."[2] Stress has ruined many relationships and many lives. Stress not only happens; it hurts. Perhaps some of my readers could be writing this chapter, telling how stress has cost them their

[2] Kenneth H. Cooper, M.D., *Can Stress Heal?* Nashville, TN: Thomas Nelson Publishers, 1997, p23.

health, their happiness, their homes, and in many cases their hopes.

James was writing these words to those who knew a great deal about stress. They were, as we have noticed, the scattered ones who had lost their homes, their jobs, and their belongings, yet James told them to consider it pure joy when they fell into "various trials" (James 1:2). (The Greek word translated "various" is *poikilos* meaning "many colored" or "many kinds.") James knew that trials are not all alike. Some of them are job related, some are financial in nature, some are domestic, and some are the result of the fear of failure. Other trials are the result of old age, guilt, competition at school or at work, problems at the office or day-by-day experiences in the home. The point is, we are faced with trials of all sorts and stripes. Some trials are natural. They come from sickness, accident, disappointment, or other painful circumstances. These trials are natural because we live in fleshly bodies and in a sinful world. Other trials are supernatural. They come upon us because we're Christians. Peter reminded us that we should "not be surprised at the painful trial you're suffering, as though something strange were happening to you" (I Pet. 4:12). Often when we line up with Christ, we line up against the present world system.

Stress in ministry manifests itself in many ways; not the least of which is a rising epidemic of unhealthy pastors. Pastors today minister in a world that knows the stress and fear and preoccupation of the possibility of further terrorists' attacks that can have devastating results on us whether they be chemical or biological. However, the United States Surgeon General, Dr. Richard Carmona, recently warned that "people should not lose sight of the nation's biggest health threat: being overweight" (*Dallas Morning News*, January 24, 2003). The Surgeon General went on to say that "the fastest growing cause of illness and death in America today is being overweight or obese." He noted that 300,000 die annually of health complications stemming directly from being overweight. According to the attorney general's office, two out of three Americans are overweight or obese, a 50% increase from a decade ago. Dr. Carmona asserted that "we are a treatment oriented society. We wait for people to get sick, and then we spend top dollar to make them healthy again."

In a recent *USA Today* article, it was reported that being overweight raises the risk of heart disease, diabetes and arthritis. There is also evidence that overweight and obese men and women have a higher risk of death from most types of cancers, including cancer of the esophagus, colon, liver, pancreas and kidneys. Eugenia Calle of the American Cancer Society stated, "We are at the same point now with obesity that we were with smoking in the mid-'60s. We made smoking cessation a national priority as a society then, and we need to make maintaining a healthy weight a national priority now."

The truth that stress is problematic is apparent in our health insurance program for Southern Baptist ministers. The number one and number two medical claims paid in 2002 were for musculoskeletal and circulatory issues. That is, such ailments as back problems and high blood pressure and the like. Both of these issues are what can be defined in many cases as "preventable diseases." They are often the result of being overweight and living a sedentary lifestyle. These two issues alone amounted to almost one fourth of our entire paid claims and when other preventable issues such as digestive and nervous conditions are included, the result approaches forty percent of our total claims paid. In addition, our number one and number two prescriptions supplied to our ministers in 2002 were for gastrodigestive issues directly related to stress. There is no question about the fact that stress is not only predictable but it is problematic in ministry today. One of the biggest needs for pastors today is to learn how to eat healthy and exercise regularly. Studies show that each additional unnecessary pound of fat contains over 200 miles of blood vessels and capillaries which cause stress on the heart because it has to work that much harder to pump blood.

In a recent letter to me a Texas pastor shared how he was challenged to do something about his health. "On June 12, 2002, my wife and I were celebrating our 20th wedding anniversary at the Southern Baptist Convention in St. Louis, Missouri," he said. "On that date you spoke about the rising cost of health care, stating a primary factor for this surge was that individuals are increasingly becoming more and more overweight. As I sat next to my wife and thought of our 20 wonderful years of marriage and the three children God has blessed us with, I heard your words and did an evaluation of my life. I came to realize that due to my size, I had become a part of the problem. I returned home and began a comprehensive exercise and health program."

He shared that just two months later, a member of his church approached him about training to run a marathon in January of 2003. "At first I laughed," he said. "then agreed to think about it before I said 'no,' but I was sure it would be impossible for me to train to run a marathon in such a short period of time. As I thought and prayed about this impossibility, God gave me a verse of scripture to base my future on. Hebrews 12:11 says, 'No discipline seems pleasant at the time, but painful. Later on, however, it produces a harvest of righteousness and peace for those who have been trained by it.' "Armed with this scripture and a determination that only God could provide, I said 'yes' and began running four to five times per week."

"At first I struggled to run any distance longer than a mile without stopping," he said. "But God has masterfully crafted the human body in such a way that it responds amazingly fast to regular periods of physical activity. Before I knew it, my long runs moved beyond three miles, to five, then eight, then 10, and on up the mileage went. I will never forget the day I ran 10 miles without stopping. Every step of the way I realized God was bringing to pass what He had promised in His Word.

"On January 19, 2003 at 7 a.m., the moment I had sweated and trained for had arrived. As the cannon sounded that morning, I said a prayer and began to run. My goal was to complete my first marathon in less than five hours. Four hours and 54 minutes later I crossed the finish line feeling great and very, very pleased."

"I have lost over 40 pounds to date with the complete expectation of losing another 25 over the next three to four months. My resting heart rate has dropped from 74 to approximately 50 beats per minute. Although I have never had to take blood pressure medicine, my blood pressure sometimes ran borderline high, but not any more. It is completely normal. On top of this, I feel better than I have in years and am better able to serve God's purposes for my life. Because of God's strength, I am achieving a goal that has eluded me for over 19 years. God bless you for challenging me to be all I can be for His Kingdom!"

Obesity is keeping many pastors today from being all they can be for God. I often wonder if Jesus looked at many modern ministers today He might not say, "By this shall all men know you are my disciples...that you're not taking care of your body which is my temple." It seems that the secular community is sounding the alarm over the evils of obesity but Christian churches do not seem to have heard the message. Periodically the Annuity Board conducts studies about the health of our ministers. In 1997 we conducted a study of ministers attending the Southern Baptist Convention in Dallas. Of 969 people surveyed, 60% of the ministers and their spouses were overweight. More than 47% were in the obese category. The problem lies not simply with the quantity of food we eat but with the quality of food that we eat. Our studies show that a small percentage eat breakfast and 61% reported they eat doughnuts and pastries, foods high in fat with little nutritional value. Forty-eight percent eat lunch in fast-food restaurants more than once a week. Seventy-five percent report eating fried foods for dinner, their largest meal, at least four nights a week. Forty percent of our ministers snack two or more times a day on cookies, chips, or candy. We're pretty good at avoiding alcohol and tobacco but 25% of us drink six or more cups of coffee a day. Baptists definitely hold the heavyweight title in ministry. High anxiety in our high calling — stress on the job, may very well be the major culprit.

"I used to be very active, running a couple of miles a day," reported a bi-vocational pastor, "but as the rigors of bi-vocational ministry became more stressful, the less time I had for exercise. As my exercise routine fell to the wayside, my weight became a problem," he said. "A year ago I was diagnosed with Type II diabetes. I don't know that I'd say stress caused the illness, however stress did make it more difficult for me to eat right and exercise. The diagnosis of diabetes has drastically changed every part of my health," he continued. "Now I'm very careful to eat right and exercise. I try to avoid fast foods whenever possible. The healthier I eat, the better my moods, and the less fatigue can set in."

When we have high levels of stress we tend to eat more. Let's face it, pastors are hounded by work pressures. If the church is not growing, the finger of accusation is usually pointed at the pastor. Many of our pastors are barely making it on what the church pays them. Low morale and low compensation add to the stress level of ministers in ministry. All of this results in an eating epidemic which has tremendous implications on our health. Yes, stress can be problematic.

One pastor's story tells how his stress level got so bad that he ended up leaving the pastorate. "I spent 11 years in public accounting and two in oil and gas accounting and management so I was used to high stress. But the pastorate is a different kind of stress. You serve the Lord and He is the One you answer to, but there are hundreds of people you minister to on a weekly basis to whom you also are accountable," he said. "Your stress arises out of the multiple responsibilities you have in the ministry, each one with its own stress points — staff, committees, building campaigns, finances, death and funerals, hospitals and illnesses, three fresh sermons a week, counseling on a wide range of problems, quarrels among church members, business meetings, deacons meetings, budget issues, special events, community involvement, special worship services, etc. The ministry raises the minister's stress level to new highs and that often affects his health in negative ways."

This pastor went on to explain that the schedule he tried to keep worked against him physically. He didn't get enough sleep or exercise, and he often found himself eating on the run and "stress eating."

"I gained weight, was more sedentary than ever before, and began to dread the things that once brought me incredible happiness and joy," he explained. "And I began to experience bouts of depression with the feeling that it wasn't going to get better. I began to look for a way out.

"Unfortunately, I waited too long to make significant lifestyle changes to remain in the pastorate," he continued. "But after leaving and joining a Southern Baptist agency, I began to see that there was hope to get my life back. As I listened to other pastors and staff members talk about the same problems I was experiencing, I realized they needed help now, before they reached the point of leaving their ministries.

"I was now looking at my life from a different perspective and realized I needed to exercise and get some of my weight off. After going to my doctor and getting my blood work done, I started on a new way of eating.

"First, it was important for me to realize that whatever I did, I needed a lifestyle change. I didn't need to just lose pounds, I needed to change my eating and exercise habits for life," he said. "I also needed to accept that I would have ups and downs through the whole process, but my commitment was for a permanent change. With that in mind, in addition to dieting, I began a regimen of walking an hour a day, five days a week. Six months into the diet and exercise program, I went back to my doctor and had my blood work done a second time to make sure all the indicators were going in the right direction. Everything was moving along well, 1 was losing weight and my cholesterol was down in the right balance between good and bad cholesterol. So I continued.

"After one year, I went back to the doctor and had my blood work done a third time," he said. "Everything was still moving in the right direction. I had lost over 50 pounds, my cholesterol had come down significantly and I felt great. I now drink more water, no caffeine, take in very little sugar and still walk one hour a day three to five times a week."

Dr. Ken Cooper reveals how all of these intense pressures and stresses associated with ministry can in fact trigger the release of certain "stress hormones." These chemical secretions include adrenaline (epinephrine) and noradrenaline (norepinephrine), which are produced by the adrenals, the endocrine glands located next to the kidneys. Typically, adrenaline floods the body when a person is fearful or anxious, with the result that certain blood channeling capillaries are shut down: hence, the paleness that comes to one's face when the blood is squeezed away from the skin. In contrast, the levels of non-adrenaline increase dramatically when a person becomes angry, and the chemical reactions can cause the face and neck to become flushed. Among other things the blood vessels constrict, causing the heart to pump faster and producing other changes known as the "fight or flight" response. Such chemical changes were originally designed to prepare the body to handle straightforward challenges, such as responding to a weapon wielding human enemy or fending off attacks of wild beasts. In other words, these adrenaline rushes either helped us to run away or stand our ground and fight. When this happens, the heart beats faster and blood pressure rises. Stress causes blood to be shunted from the stomach and skin to the muscles to provide physical strength for a fight or flight. Our blood sugar level begins to rise, breathing quickens, our eyes may dilate, and chemicals appear in the blood to clot blood rapidly in case of emergency. The body is an amazing and miraculous creation. Its heightened development may well serve to save our body but it definitely has enormous consequences also. This is what happens when we hear incidences of people being able to use superhuman strength, like, for example, lifting a car off someone in a time of emergency. This is also what enables the kid in the schoolyard who is cornered by the class bully to come out swinging. All of these reactions are normal reactions as our body relates to stress. The problem comes when we do not fight or flee and are left to deal with these lingering physical issues.

There are several indicators which help to identify stress in our lives. There are physical signs. Such things as tension, headaches, back pain, change of appetite, change in sleep habits, and higher blood pressure are often warning signs that stress is building within us. There are also behavioral signs. These may include a loss of productivity, strained relationships, loss of concentration, overeating, compulsive behavior, and the like. Some of the most obvious signs begin to appear in the emotional realm. These may well include such things as depression, a loss of self worth, a feeling of failure, frustration, withdrawal and/or isolation. Then, of course, there are spiritual signs such as a loss of a devotional life, a loss of focus and concentration in our prayer lives, and a loss of passion and concern for a lost world around us.

Ignoring these warning signs gives rise to the fact that stress is problematic. It can trigger a heart attack. It can result in excess stomach acid which produces ulcers. It definitely lends itself to high blood pressure resulting from continued stress. In short, fear, anxiety, and worry causes the brain to command the adrenaline gland to inject strong chemicals into our blood stream. These chemicals act as a poison over an extended period of time, which is why continued stress on the part of our ministers can be extremely problematic. Consequently, it is no surprise that among the thousands upon thousands of Baptist ministers in our insurance program the number one and two medications prescribed this past year were for stress related illnesses. Yes, stress is problematic.

While much of the above conversation relates to the minister it should not be forgotten that many pastors' wives are suffering in silence. The pastor's family is under a tremendous amount of stress in many ways and places today. Pastors are constantly attempting to juggle the demands of ministry and family. One survey I heard about recently from Dr. H. B. London of Focus on the Family said that 53% of pastors' wives are "in some sort of depression." While their husbands are going through their own kinds of ministry stress, their wives are suffering and so often suffering silently. It is easy to see why so many ministerial families are in crisis. Stress can be problematic.

Perhaps there is no better biblical illustration of how stress can affect a man of God than is found in I Kings 19 with the familiar story of Elijah. Here was, indisputably, one of the mightiest men of the Bible. However, after his great victory on Mt. Carmel we find him a few verses later completely stressed out and fleeing for his life. It is a fallacy to think that only those who are failures suffer from stress. Few men in history have risen to the success and achievement of Elijah in such a short period of time. In many ways stress leads us to depression as it did this mighty man of God. While some are depressed because of biochemical changes in their bodies, many are down-trodden for the same reasons as Elijah.

The stress brought on by the ministry can result in burnout for a pastor. "Burnout and depression can be hard to distinguish as two separate problems," said one former pastor. "I think burnout is one of the possible results of unchecked depression."

"I can now see what I couldn't see while I was pastoring," he explained. "I can look back now and realize that I had no defense in place to handle the intense stress of the pastorate. I was doing nothing to protect myself. Had I been conscious of the problems and countered them with exercise, good eating habits and a strong support group, I probably would not have reached the burnout stage that I did."

He went on to say that by nature of the ministry to which they are called, ministers face intense stress and often certain levels of depression. "But God didn't intend for it to beat us, but rather to drive us closer to Him," he said. "We have to take care of these bodies and thus our ministries. Since I've been eating better and getting regular exercise, I feel much better physically, but just as important, I feel much better mentally and spiritually."

Now, back to Elijah for a moment. There were several sources of stress in the life of Elijah. First there was forgetfulness (I Kin. 19:1–3). He'd just come down from the mountain of great victory at Mt. Carmel where he had believed God in spite of what seemed to be. It is always dangerous after a great victory. Elijah began to think that yesterday's victories would suffice for today's commitments and forgetfulness became a source of his stress. He took his eyes off God and put them on wicked Queen Jezebel who was out for his life. Some of us fall into stress for the very same reason, that is, forgetfulness. Like Elijah we too have seen God come through in our behalf but then when the crisis comes, when a Jezebel knocks at our own door, sometimes we forget God and run away.

Another source of his stress was fear (I Kin. 19:1–3). Fear is not an action, it is a reaction. It's like faith. Faith is also a reaction instead of an action. When the crisis comes and our lives are governed by situations and circumstances, our reaction will be fear. However, when the crisis comes and our life is governed by scripture, our reaction will be faith. Some suffer from stress because outward circumstances dictate that they not only are forgetful but they also have fear.

Another source of Elijah's stress was fatigue (I Kin. 19:3). He had just spent many hours on top of Mt. Carmel. The emotional stress was unbelievable. Then to top it off he ran from Jezebel all the way down to Beersheba, a distance of over 100 miles. He was exhausted. No wonder he collapsed with fatigue under the juniper tree. Fatigue is the plague of modern ministry today. It often keeps us from thinking right and making proper decisions. It is one of the major sources of stress.

A final source of stress was failure (I Kin. 19:1–3). Elijah, although he had been so successful in the past, now felt he was a failure. All of these sources — forgetfulness, fear, fatigue — led him to frustration and failure and a give-up kind of an attitude.

Elijah is not only a good illustration of the sources of stress but also of the symptoms of stress. There's a distinction between the sources of a problem and the symptoms of a problem. Much of our difficulty is found in treating symptoms and not sources. Once these sources lead us to stress, there are some symptoms that show us where we really are and cause us to hear the alarm. The first is detachment (I Kin. 19:4). That is, isolation, withdrawal. This is one of the first symptoms of stress. Elijah left those who loved him most and detached himself. Remember, this is a symptom and not a source. People try to deal with stress by treating symptoms so they try all sorts of positive thinking to get back on track. Another symptom of stress is despondency (I Kin. 19:4), that is, helplessness, pessimism. Elijah had lost his will to live. He wasn't thinking right because he was allowing fear and fatigue to rule his mind. He sat down under a juniper tree completely stressed out. A third symptom of stress is defeat (I Kin. 19:4). We see him sitting under the tree contemplating suicide in self-depreciation and with a defeatist attitude. In essence he is saying, "I am worthless." Remember, this is not the source of depression, it is simply a symptom. There is also the element of deception (I Kin. 19:10–18). Here we see the faulty thinking that results from a stress filled life. Elijah thought he was the only one left still standing for God and God reminded him that He had thousands who had not bowed their knee to the false god, Baal. How easy it is when we become stressed to not think correctly. Finally, defensiveness is a telltale symptom of stress. Elijah became preoccupied with self, became defensive of anything else and everyone else. These are telltale symptoms of a stress filled life — detachment, despondency, defeat, deception, and defensiveness.

We also see in the life of Elijah some solutions to stress. There are the physical solutions (I Kin. 19:5–7). The first thing Elijah did to overcome his stress was to eat properly and sleep properly. This is some of the greatest advice he can give to many of our pastors today. "I find that I experience less fatigue and frustration when I take care of myself," one bi-vocational pastor said. "I have much more energy to commit to both my ministry and my full-time job. Sensible eating, along with regular exercise, has given me the energy I need to complete the tasks ahead of me. God is my strength," he continued, "but taking steps to avoid stress helps sustain me to do what I have been called to do." One of the very first things we ought to do to overcome stress in our lives is to eat a properly balanced diet and get plenty of rest. The solution is partly physical. Every minister who sees in his own life these symptoms and sources of stress should see his personal physician and seek his doctor's counsel and advice.

The solution is not only physical it is also personal (I Kin. 19:9–12). God comes to Elijah and asks him a very important question as he moves from his juniper tree to his place of isolation in his cave — "What are you doing here?" I've always wondered where God put the inflection in His voice when He asked that question. Did He say, "What are YOU doing here?" Elijah, you had such courage, such faith, what are YOU doing here? Or, did God ask, "What are you doing HERE?" Have you ever been in a place where you knew God did not want you to be? Perhaps He phrased the question in the following manner — "What are you DOING here?" Elijah had to answer, "I'm not doing anything, Lord." Many lose their joy by doing nothing. Yes, the solution is personal. God said, "Go and stand on the mountain." Elijah did and there he heard "the still small voice." There are times when we are so stressed we have to get under the juniper tree so we can hear God speak. I suppose the great lessons of life are not learned on the mountains but are learned in the valleys. It is there where we beat out in the practical experience of life, the spiritual lessons that lead us on to victory.

Not only is the solution to stress physical and personal, it is also practical (I Kin. 19:15–16). God gave Elijah a new task and a new job. It involved other people. It was a very practical solution. Elijah went from here to the greatest days of his ministry. Our stress does not have to be a dead end. It may be a turn in the road that winds ever upward. Stress is problematic but it does not have to be our foe, it can be turned into our friend.

Although stress can be problematic, there is hope. We should find comfort in the fact that the stress is transitory. Peter said, "In this you greatly rejoice, though now *for a little while*, if need be, you have been grieved by various trials" (I Pet. 1:6, italics added). One of the most common phrases in the Bible simply says, "And it came to pass." Are you faced with the stress of trials right now? This too shall pass! It is transitory. Perhaps Longfellow said it best when he said, "The lowest ebb is the turn of the tide." In my office hangs a beautiful painting of a sunset with these inscribed words: "There's never been a sunset yet not followed by a sunrise."

Stress can certainly be problematic. More so than anyone else, those who have received the high calling of the ministry should find a renewed emphasis in having the witness of a healthy body. Paul reminds us our bodies are "the temples of the Holy Spirit" (I Cor. 6:19–20). Interestingly, he used the word *naos* which we translate "temple" in this verse. The New Testament translates two different words into one English word "temple". One describes the inner sanctuary, the Holy of Holies in the temple. The other describes the entire temple mount. Paul uses the former word here. He is saying that our bodies are the holy of holies; that innermost holy place. In the Old Testament God had a temple for His people but in the New Testament He has a people for His temple. You are the dwelling place of the Holy Spirit!

Paul continues in this same passage to remind us that we are "bought with a price." The Greek word means that it refers to something precious. God went into the marketplace and bought us for a very expensive price. This very fact ought to do something about our own self-image and spur us on to take care of our bodies which are in fact the dwelling place of the Spirit of God Himself.

Paul then concludes the passage by saying, "Therefore glorify God in your body." It is important to note that we are to honor God with something specific here, our bodies.

One employee at the Annuity Board found out the hard way the high price of not honoring her body. In December of 2000, she was diagnosed with Type II diabetes. "I knew that if I didn't change my health habits, my life would be at risk," she said. In February of 2001, she began a walking program. "At first I was walking 15 to 20 minutes a day," she said. "Gradually I increased the time to 30 and then 60 minutes per day." After 11 months, she had lost a total of 60 pounds and her doctor eliminated her blood pressure and diabetes medication. This individual now monitors her weight with daily exercise and a low fat, sugar-free diet. "In a way, finding out about the diabetes saved my life," she explained. "I believe this was God's way of giving me a wake-up call to take care of my body before my body could no longer take care of me." We have a spiritual stewardship that needs to be quickened in our own priorities of life.

Stress does not have to be as problematic as it is. In fact, it can be used to our advantage when we see that in a very real sense it is not only predictable and problematic, but as we shall see in the next chapter, it can also be paradoxical.

Chapter 3

Stress is paradoxical

(James 1:2–4)

James says we should "count it all joy" when we face trials of many kinds. Count it what? Joy! How much joy? All joy! Could this be a misprint? Most of us consider various kinds of stressful trials to be a taste of hell itself, not all joy. We generally count it all joy when we avoid trials and stressful tribulations. We hear about someone else's stressful trial and breathe a prayer of joyful thanks that we are not faced with the same problem.

Talk about a paradox! James' admonition seems diametrically opposed to the way we would naturally look at difficulties. His advice certainly seems strange on the surface. Most of us would say, "Count it all joy when you *escape* trials of various kinds." For 15 years my family and I lived in South Florida in what is often called "hurricane alley." Every single year during hurricane season we would do our best to hopefully dodge the massive variety of storms that would make their way westward across the ocean toward us. We would consider it joy when we escaped those kinds of trials. But here James is telling the believer that, paradoxically, he should count it all joy when he falls into various stressful ordeals.

In his book, *The Joy of Stress*, Dr. Peter Hanson reminds us that stress in not necessarily our enemy at all. He, like James of old, tells us that rather than challenging people to avoid stress it is far better to see stress as a friend and not a foe and learn to handle it in such a way that something good can come from it. Often, some of the most stressful jobs are those for which we are not suited. Ministers have a high calling. There is something supernatural about what we do and where we do it. God still calls particular people to particular places for particular purposes. However, just because we have a high calling does not mean that it is not filled with high anxiety from time to time. Times of stress should be times of making sure we're in the midst of God's will doing what He called us to do and being where He called us to be. There is, according to Dr. Hanson, a real sense in which stress is not a four-letter word but something that is actually neutral in our lives. Our reactions to it and not our actions are often the issue. After all, Jesus preached the whole Sermon on the Mount to show us the importance of our reactions as necessarily opposed to our actions. He said when stressful circumstances and situations arise, such as someone slapping us on the cheek, that it is the reaction that matters most. He said when some stressful circumstance comes our way as when someone steals our coat then it is our reaction that matters most. Yes, stress is paradoxical. We can indeed "count it all joy when we fall into various trials."

The Greek word that is translated here in James 1:2, instructing us to "count it" all joy, is in the aorist tense which signifies that the joy that we read about comes after the trial. James is not saying the trial is joy. He is not advocating some type of sadomasochism here. The word means to "think ahead, to think forward." Job was thinking ahead when he said, "But He knows the way that I take and when He has tested me I will come forth as gold" (Job 23:10). Job did not consider losing his health a joy. But he looked forward to the joy that would follow his trial.

Joseph also counted it all joy — he thought ahead. When revealing his identity to his brothers after so many years of hurt he said, "You intended to harm me but God intended it for good to accomplish what is now being done, the saving of many lives" (Gen. 50:20). Did Joseph count it all joy to be in prison? Of course not. But he knew God's hand was in his circumstances and he was thinking ahead.

And what about our Lord? Jesus looked beyond his suffering. Hebrews 12:2 says that it was "for the joy that was set before Him that He endured the cross, despising the shame, and is sat down at the right hand of the throne of God" (Heb. 12:2). Did Jesus count Calvary a joy? Certainly not! But thinking ahead, He thought past Calvary and therefore He bore up under the stress of the cross. Do you get the point?

Can you, like Job or Joseph or Jesus, think ahead in the midst of your circumstance and situation? Have you considered it joy to be in the midst of a stressful situation? James is not saying that we have joy in the midst of our trials, but that we have joy at what lies ahead. It seems paradoxical, but James is saying, "There can be joy in the outcome."

While writing this chapter I flew at thirty thousand feet in route to a speaking engagement. I saw James 1:2 come alive on the airplane. I was seated next to a woman who by all appearances was sophisticated, beautiful, and charming. She seemed to have everything the world has to offer. But as we conversed she explained that though her husband had inherited the family fortune in business, he was hooked on cocaine. He had just spent six weeks in a treatment center in Virginia, and she was about to see him for the first time in a month and a half. She had talked with him the previous day by telephone and he had said that the counselors at the treatment center had told him that he needed to believe in "some higher power." It was my great joy to share with her who that "higher power" is and how she can know Him personally and receive the free pardoning of sin and the gift of eternal life. Before we landed — with tears streaming down her face, yet with a countenance of joy — she invited Jesus Christ to be her personal Savior and Lord. Yes, she could now consider it pure joy as she faced her trial and stress.

The Apostle Paul wrote, "For our light affliction, which is but for a moment, is working for us a far more exceeding and eternal weight of glory, while we do not look at the things which are seen, but at the things which are not seen. For the things which are seen are temporary but the things that are not seen are eternal" (II Cor. 4:17–18).

In his classic book, *Can Stress Heal?*, Dr. Kenneth Cooper of the famed Aerobic Center and Cooper Clinic in Dallas devotes a whole section of the book to what he calls, "the great paradox of stress." Dr. Cooper says, "Paradoxically, the very work that can on occasion stress me out is also one of my most significant sources of satisfaction. I tend to take on too much not because I'm a masochist, driven to inflict pain on my body and psyche, but because I really love what I do." He goes on to say, "In practical terms, my personal fight against stress — which I also call my 'stress immunization' — involves seven steps. These constitute the basics of the paradox prescription program that I recommend to my patients. They are:

Step 1: Assume a paradoxical mindset (this is exactly what James is saying when he challenges us to count it all joy when we fall into various trials).

Step 2: Build a foundation of healthy sleep.

Step 3: Take regular doses of nature's best tranquilizer — aerobic and other physical exercise.

Step 4: Learn to fight stress on the molecular level. (At this point we should seek medical help as to the dangerous disturbance of the delicate balance of hormones, common chemicals and other micro components deep inside our bodies. There are all sorts of chemical changes that occur in our bodies and emotions during and after stressful circumstances and situations.)

Step 5: Effect a powerful mind-spirit defense perimeter. (Dr. Cooper, a powerful follower of Jesus Christ deals here with the importance of not simply the physical but the spiritual dimension in overcoming stressful circumstances and situations.)

Step 6: Become an expert in using "depressurizing tactics in daily high stress situations." (This primarily involves releasing, letting go of certain circumstances and also retreating from our work, that is, coming apart so that we might not come apart.)

Step 7: Get regular medical stress check-ups.

Noting Dr. Cooper's emphasis on the spiritual it is also important to note that James is addressing those whom he calls "my brethren" (James 1:2). The Greek word, *adelphoi*, indicates that James is writing to those who are sharing a mutual life. His readers were brothers in the faith. It is folly to tell a lost man to consider it pure joy when he faces stressful trials of many kinds. He will probably look at you as though you were crazy. This perspective on stress is only for those in the family of God and is closely related to the family secret we find in Romans 8:28: "For we know that all things work together for the good to those who love God and are called according to his purpose." This is a family secret. When asked to quote this verse most people leave off the first phrase — "and we know." The lost world certainly does not know the truth of Romans 8:28. It is indeed a family secret. However, we (those of us in the family of God) certainly know it to be true. It is no wonder that we can count it all joy when we fall into various stressful trials.

Every stressful trial can become a God given opportunity for growing in the likeness of Jesus Christ. Oswald Chambers, the great devotional writer of a past generation, once said, "Every humiliation, everything that tries and vexes us, is God's way of cutting a deeper channel through us in which the life of Christ can flow." Yes, the stress of trials is paradoxical. James said that we should consider it joy because it is used to bring us into spiritual maturity. He goes on to say, "Knowing that the testing of your faith produces patience, let patience have its perfect work, that you may be perfect and complete, lacking nothing" (James 1:3–4).

Chapter 4

Stress is purposeful

(James 1:3–8)

James now reminds us that stress is not simply pre-dictable, problematic, and paradoxical but it can also be purposeful. He reminds us in James 1:3–8 that it produces purity, perseverance, perfection and prayer.

Stress is purposeful. It produces *purity*. One ultimate purpose of stress is to lead us to purity. James reminds us that "the testing of your faith produces patience." In the Greek New Testament the word we translate "testing" is the word *dokimion*. It is also found in I Peter 1:7 where it is translated "proved." Peter wrote that various trials come our way "so that the genuineness of your faith being much more precious than gold that perishes, though it is tested by fire, may be found to the praise, honor, and glory at the revelation of Jesus Christ."

This particular Greek word can also be translated "purging." The word conveys a picture of a precious metal being heated until it is liquid and its impurities rise to the top and are scraped off. Only pure metal is left. The word also conveys the picture of the lady who goes to a fabric store, picks up a piece of fabric, and pulls it one way and then another to see if it will take the proper strain. By using *dokimion* James emphasizes that stress tests our faith. Our trials are for a purpose. Often they are a refining fire, testing us to see if we can hold up under pressure and thus conforming us to the image of Christ. How many of us in ministry can look back over times of high anxiety and see that they ultimately were allowed as a refining fire and we discovered for ourselves that stress truly was purposeful and that it produced purity in our own lives.

My high school chemistry teacher, Prof. Dunkelberg, was always giving us pop quizzes. Why? To prove our ability. To help us learn and grow. It is the same in the school of faith. God's purpose is for us to reach graduation day, so He allows tests along the way. And so often, just like many of my teacher's pop tests, they are unexpected and in many cases unwelcome. However, God has a purpose and a plan behind it all. Stress can be purposeful in that it can produce purity in our lives.

It also produces *perseverance*. James said that the testing of our faith develops patience or perseverance. The word here is derived in Greek from a preposition which means "under" and a verb that means "to stand fast." Thus, James is saying that the testing of our faith develops the staying power that will help us to stand up under other tests. The King James translators chose the word "patience," but that is a weak translation. *Hupomeno* is a much stronger word which more appropriately is translated, "endurance," "steadfastness" or "perseverance." *Hupomeno* evokes a picture of someone under pressure who stands his ground instead of escaping.

Only a trial can prove the depth of our faith and character. Note what is being tested. What is on trial here? Are we? No. Our faith! James is talking about the testing of our faith. Many people misunderstand the book of James, falsely thinking that it is an epistle of works. But before James ever mentions works, he talks much about faith. It is our faith which is put to the test. The Bible says, "Without faith it is impossible to please God" (Heb. 11:6). There are a lot of men and women serving their high calling in the midst of high anxiety. There are many who are undergoing the process of testing, *dokimion*. The heat is on. The thermostat is turned up. Remember, the stress of trials has a purpose. It can produce purity and perseverance in your life. God is perfecting you and you will come out stronger and sturdier than ever with the ability to "stand up under" what comes your way.

Another purpose of stress is that it leads us to *perfection*. In fact, stress can produce perfection. James says, "Let patience have its perfect work that you may be perfect and complete lacking nothing" (James 1:4). Why must perseverance finish its work? So that we might be "perfect" or "mature." The word means, "to end, to carry work to its end, to become full-grown."

The word picture is of a student who goes to school to earn a diploma. Along the way he may fail a few tests, miss a few math problems, confuse a few historical facts and dates. But all of that is incidental to finishing the course and walking across the stage to receive his diploma on graduation day. In the school of stressful trials we fail a few tests along the way and perhaps confuse a few facts. But all along the way God is making us ready, maturing and completing us for that day when we will walk across the heavenly stage to receive our spiritual diplomas.

Our goal in Christian living is spiritual maturity. Yet, learning to mature brings danger and risks. There are a lot of tests along the way. I remember when our oldest daughter turned 16 and it was time to teach her how to drive. (Some of our greatest private times together took place on Saturday afternoons in a big empty parking lot where she learned to drive.) The time finally came when she obtained her driver's license and headed out on her own. The only way she could mature in her driving was for her mother and me to release her and that involved risks. The same is true of spiritual maturity. The one who never undergoes stressful trials will never mature in the faith. Stress is purposeful.

Stress not only produces purity, perseverance, and perfection, it also produces *prayer*. No wonder we say it is purposeful! James 1:5 puts it like this, "If any of you lacks wisdom, let him ask of God who gives to all liberally and without reproach and it will be given to him." The Greek word for wisdom used here (*sophia*) means "the practical use of knowledge." It has been defined as the ability to discern God's hand in human circumstances and apply heavenly judgment to earthly situations.

This was the burden of Paul's prayer for the church at Ephesus. "I keep asking," he wrote, "that the God of our Lord Jesus Christ, the glorious Father, may give you the spirit of wisdom" (Eph. 1:17). It was also his prayer for the Colossians, "We have not stopped praying for you and asking God to fill you with the knowledge of His will through all spiritual wisdom and understanding" (Col. 1:9).

This kind of wisdom is not simply knowledge. We can read every book ever written on stress and still not know how to cope. We do not need to pray to be smart, but to be wise. People going through stressful trials need Godly wisdom more than anything else. When we go through trials, we have a tendency to lose perspective and direction. It becomes so easy to take our focus off the Lord and put our focus on circumstances or people; we forget that the wisdom we need originates with God.

The greatest need of modern man is wisdom (*sophia*). Think about this with me. In many ways our generation is the most progressive of all generations. We have more college graduates. In our day and age it is not enough simply to have a bachelor's degree. It is increasingly important to have graduate degrees to excel in our chosen professions. Knowledge is exploding. We travel farther and fly higher and faster than any previous generation in history. We accumulate data as never before. The computer age continues to advance in such a way that information becomes outdated with virtually every passing day. But while such knowledge is increasing, wisdom is often lacking. Many of our lives are in shambles. Suicide rates are higher than ever before. More are dropping out of ministry than at any time in recent history. Morals are at a record low. In many ways our whole world seems on the brink of chaos. And to such a generation James 1:5 says, "If any of you lacks wisdom he should ask of God."

To whom does God give this wisdom, this supernatural, divine discernment? James says that He gives it to those who ask. We do not get *sophia* in school or from practical experience. It is God's gift to us. God is a giving God and He is not stingy with wisdom. He gives it "liberally," in the words of James. However, we must ask for it. James used a present active imperative form of the Greek word for "ask." This means that we are to "keep on asking." Our requests are not just to be shots in the dark, from the hip, or off the cuff. When we face stressful trials and need wisdom we are to continue to ask God for it.

James is not saying that if we lack wisdom we should sit down and think about it. No. He did not say we need to learn more about theology or keep our noses in our textbooks. He said we should "ask." This is why so many Christians lack wisdom. Some are too proud to simply ask. If God would tell us to do something hard we'd each be first in line to volunteer, but when He tells us to humble ourselves and ask for this gift, many of us balk.

When King Solomon was about to take control of the throne, God made an incredible proposition to him: "Ask for whatever you want me to give you" (I Kin. 3). Do you remember what Solomon answered? He asked for, "a discerning heart to govern his people and to distinguish between right and wrong" (I Kin. 3:9). Solomon asked for wisdom! He could have had anything he wanted, but he asked for wisdom. He chose the best, and God threw in the rest. Here is the scenario. You have a crisis. It creates stress. So what do you do? Call the doctor and order some more pills? Make another appointment with a counselor? Go out and buy some self-help books? Or, do you pray? Often we do the best thing last. Of course there's nothing wrong with going to a doctor, seeking counsel or studying to be better. But first we should call upon God and pray. It is no coincidence that the middle verse of the Bible is Psalm 118:8 which reads, "It is better to take refuge in the Lord than to trust in man."

In his book *Can Stress Heal?*, Dr. Ken Cooper writes that a number of studies (among them a medical news article in the *Journal of the American Medical Association*, May 24–31, 1995, pp. 1561–62) have shown that a deeply held personal faith in God can reduce stress. Dr. Cooper says, "It has become apparent that a deeply felt intrinsic or inner faith can be a positive factor in health, including stress management." This learned physician goes on to say, "Perhaps the most intriguing component of the kind of faith that can produce healing — including the effective treatment of stress — is prayer." Dr. Cooper goes on to cite several different medical studies which suggest that there are many health benefits that are directly or indirectly connected to prayer.

James 4:2 says, "You do not have because you do not ask." Since the devil cannot keep God from answering our prayers, what does he do? He seeks to keep us from asking. He lies to us, often convincing some of us that we're not worthy to ask God about such things as stressful conditions. He tells us to help ourselves first and then go to God as the last resort.

Consider, for example, people under pressure at the office because of an unfair boss. If all they have to rely on is human wisdom, they will complicate the matter with confusion. They need God's wisdom to see that their situation may be orchestrated, or at least allowed by God to make them more Christ-like. The point of their friction may be allowed by God because He is working on specific parts of their lives He wants to perfect.

God gives us wisdom without finding fault. There are some people who give gifts with all sorts of strings attached, and sometimes they use the giving of these gifts as opportunities to belittle, insult, or even rebuke the recipients (as if the givers had bought the right to do so). But not God. He will never say, "You made your bed, now lie in it." He will never say, "I told you so." When we ask God for wisdom He will never look at us with crossed arms or clenched fists or pointed fingers. He will give wisdom without finding fault as James says.

How we ask is also important. James 1:6 says, "But let him ask in faith, with no doubting, for he who doubts is like a wave of the sea driven and tossed by the wind." There is a condition attached to God's granting us wisdom. He gives it to those who ask in faith. We must believe and not doubt. The Greek word for doubt, *diakrino*, is a compound word made up of two words which mean "through" and "to separate." It conveys the sense of being divided against oneself. One incident in the life of Peter is a picture of *diakrino*. He walked on the water and then sank. Jesus said to him, "Why did you doubt?" (Matt. 14:31). He was asking, "Why did you think twice?"

We are to ask in faith. Often we hear someone say, "I asked God but nothing happened." Perhaps this particular type of person overlooks the condition: "When we ask, we must believe." No wonder Paul wrote, "We live by faith and not by sight" (II Cor. 5:7). Jesus put it like this: "Therefore I tell you, whatever you ask in prayer believe that you have received it and you will have it" (Mark 11:24). Jesus did not mean that God will give us everything for which we ask. The idea of demanding of God or "claiming" things from God is not at issue here, the issue is faith. Where is faith found? Paul says in Romans that "faith comes from hearing and hearing by the word of God" (Rom. 10:17). Faith is born of the word of God when it is quickened into our hearts by the Holy Spirit.

James likened the man who asked without faith to one who is blown by the wind and tossed by the waves. Perhaps you have been in the midst of the ocean and experienced its constant rolling. From time to time I used to fish in the Atlantic Ocean off the coast of Fort Lauderdale. When the waves were rolling it was difficult to keep the boat on course. Likewise, doubt leaves one unsettled. If we want smooth sailing through life, we must believe that God knows what is best for us, and by faith ask Him for wisdom.

The doubting man has no sense of direction in life. James 1:7–8 says, "For let not that man suppose that he will receive anything from the Lord; he is a double-minded man, unstable in all his ways." The one who doubts will not receive wisdom from the Lord. Rather, he will simply be the victim of greater stress. Ineffective prayers are due in part to what James referred to as "double-mindedness." The word means two thought patterns, with a soul divided between faith and the world. The doubting man has a divided heart. He is trying to serve two masters. It is as though a part of him shouts, "I believe" and the other part cries out, "I doubt." James says that this type of individual is unstable in all he does. In other words, doubt affects every area of our lives. Unstable in his relationship with God, he cannot live by faith and is therefore unstable at home, in the workplace, social situations, and everywhere else. How important it is to have God's wisdom to cope with life's stresses.

Stress is purposeful. Those who serve a high calling which is filled with high anxiety must get wisdom from God in dealing and coping with the stressful pressures that come daily in ministry. It is important to keep a sense of humor. The Bible says that a merry heart does good like a medicine. It is also important to take regular time off. If our Lord sensed the need to retreat by himself as He did so often, how much more do we need to do the same in ministry today? Many pastors I know do not get nearly enough sleep, seldom if ever exercise, and eat very unbalanced and unhealthful diets. It is no wonder they are open targets to stressful circumstances and situations.

Not only is it important to keep a sense of humor and take care of ourselves physically but it goes without saying that James is emphasizing here that the spiritual dynamic of who we are and what we do is the greatest antidote to stress. It is strange how many of us in ministry fail to pray when we need it most, when we are enduring times of stress. We should all learn lessons from our Lord, the busier He became and the more stressed the circumstance and situation, the more He prayed. He also immersed Himself in the word of God. When Jesus was "stressed" in those classic temptations that are recorded in the fourth chapter of Matthew we recall how He used the word of God in standing against the stressful trials that came His way. Should we not do the same? In times of stress should we not be moved, as James challenges, to a passionate longing to deeper prayer and more devoted Bible study?

Stress can be purposeful for those in ministry who dare to be vulnerable and accountable. Life is about relationships and one of the dangers of ministry is that many pastors and church workers do not have accountable relationships which can bring synergy and support in times of stress. There are too many "Lone Rangers" riding the range of ministry.

The stress of trials is predictable, problematic, paradoxical, and purposeful. Our greatest need is wisdom. Where do we get it? We need to ask. Who gives it? God. How? In response to our faith. How will he give? Liberally.

The Psalmist put it like this, "The fear of the Lord is the beginning of wisdom" (Ps. 111:10). The man or woman who has no reverence for God is lacking true wisdom. He or she may have an IQ higher than 150, but not wisdom. Wisdom does not come from Plato nor Aristotle nor

Socrates nor Kierkegaard, nor any other philosopher of renown. Look again at the source of wisdom: "If any of you lack wisdom let him ask of God." Knowledge is the accumulation of facts. Wisdom is the ability to deal with the facts and use them in practical ways. Almost anyone can gain knowledge, but only those who seek God can gain true wisdom. Yes, for those of us in a high calling with high anxiety, stress is purposeful.

Chapter 5

Stress is profitable

(James 1:9–12)

I once heard Dr. George Sweeting, Chancellor of the Moody Bible Institute, say, "A Christian is like a teabag, he is not worth much until he has been through some hot water." Yes, trials can be profitable. James now moves on in his letter to us by describing three men: the man with poverty, the man with plenty, and the man with pressure. The trials God allows have a way of bringing all of us to one level. As a pastor, I've visited many homes to help meet the needs of families going through all sorts of stressful trials. I have driven up to million dollar waterfront homes behind big iron gates, and I have driven up to little frame homes in neighborhoods where safety requires iron bars on the windows. I've been with those in poverty, I've been with those in plenty, and I've been with those under pressure. I've seen how stress and trials have actually become profitable for those who have learned to deal with them.

Those who have heeded the high calling of ministry have found that high anxiety is prevalent everywhere. Our Southern Baptist churches run the gamut from small and rural congregations to large mega-churches in metropolitan areas. Whether one pastors in virtual poverty or with plenty, pressure comes in all shapes and sizes.

The person with poverty

James 1:9 says, "Let the lowly brother glory in his exaltation." The New International version translates this verse by saying, "The brother in humble circumstances ought to take pride in his high position." The word translated "humble" is the Greek word *tapeinos*. It means "lowly" and describes one who is low on the socioeconomic scale, one who is relatively poor and powerless. The world may think such a person is not worth much, but God says he is worth very much. Here is one of the mysteries of the Christian life: the last shall be first and the low shall be made high.

When I read James 1:9, I think of Noah. No one encouraged him. No one cheered him on. He was lampooned, mocked, laughed at, scorned, and neglected. But God exalted him!

James wrote that the brother in humble circumstances should take pride in his "exaltation" or his "high position." As followers of Christ we belong to a heavenly realm. We are of great worth to God, and we should rejoice in the spiritual things we can never lose. Our denomination is seeing an increase in Christian martyrs around the world. We are reminded of the missionary Jim Elliot who lost his life to the Auca Indians who said it best: "He is no fool who gives what he cannot keep to gain what he cannot lose."

An impoverished person must look beyond physical circumstances and abide in spiritual values. Paul did, and he wrote, "Our citizenship is in heaven where also we look for the Savior, the Lord Jesus Christ" (Phil. 3:20).

The person with plenty

The early church, like many of our churches today, had both people in poverty and people who had plenty. The fellowship included not only those in great physical and financial need, but also some of the wealthiest people in Jerusalem. There were men like Joseph of Arimathea, Nicodemus, and up in the church at Antioch there were men like Barnabas, the property owner from Cyprus.

James 1:10–11 says, "but the rich in his humiliation because as a flower of the field he will pass away. For sooner has the sun risen with the burning heat than it withers the grass; its flower falls, and its beautiful appearance perishes. So the rich man will fade away in his pursuits." Again, the New International version states the same verses like this, "The one who is rich should take pride in his low position, because he will pass away like a wild flower. For the sun rises with scorching heat and withers the plants; its blossom falls and its beauty is destroyed. In the same way the rich man will fade away even while he goes about his business." James is saying that while those who are rich according to the world standards may take pride in their possessions, the Christian person of plenty takes pride in his spiritual position. He knows that the grass withers and the flower fades, that treasures laid up on earth will rust and be devoured by moths.

For believers, poverty is temporary and so is prosperity, especially in comparison to the eternal glory that is ours in Christ Jesus. Therefore, neither poverty nor plenty makes for happiness in the Christian life. Jesus reminds us that "a man's life does not consist in the abundance of his possessions" (Luke 12:15). Those with plenty should rejoice in the spiritual things they cannot lose. If your happiness is based on your position in Christ, you can never lose that. If your happiness is found in your possessions, then you should heed James 1:11.

The man in poverty, who in the eyes of the world is not worth much, should find joy in his relationship with the Lord who elevates him to a high position. The man in plenty should remember that his only lasting security is not in stocks or bonds or properties but in his relationship with the Lord. In dealing with stress, both men should look at their lives from a heavenly perspective and not an earthly one.

The Gospel has a leveling effect. In Jericho, Jesus and his disciples met two men on the same day. One was a man in poverty and the other was a man with plenty. To Bartimaeus, the poverty-stricken, blind beggar on the roadside, Jesus said, "Rise" (Mark 10:49). To Zacchaeus, the wealthy tax collector who had climbed up in the tree, Jesus said, "Come down" (Luke 19:5). Do you see the parallel to James 1:9–10? The Gospel has always had a leveling effect on all of us.

The person with pressure

For the rich and poor alike, stress is profitable for the person under pressure. James 1:12 says, "Blessed is the man who endures temptation; for when he is approved, he will receive the crown of life which the Lord has promised to those who love Him." Satan wants to use stressful trials to cause us to stumble, but God allows them in order for us to stand. The word "endures," or "perseveres" in some translations, is the verb form of the noun we earlier saw in James 1:3. It means "staying power." Perseverance is not the morbid response of a person who sits down, bows his head, and passively endures rebukes and testings. Perseverance is the response of the person who bears up under stressful circumstances. Perhaps you find yourself buried under trials at this time. What should you do? Some say you should run away. But James' advice was "stand up under them." Hold your ground!

When we speak of the person with pressure there are few vocations as pressure packed as vocational ministry today. The pastor is under weekly pressure to prepare two or three fresh and relevant messages with good content. There is the pressure to build and maintain relationships, sometimes with difficult people. The ministry is the people business and some people can be downright difficult. There is also the pressure that comes from listening to people's problems day after day. There is the pressure that results in not having a pastor ourselves or someone with whom we can bare our soul. The pressure of leadership and setting the pace for varied ministries is constantly present. Along with this is the continual pressure to maintain and build momentum in a myriad of church ministries. And then, not the least of all is the pressure of guarding precious and valuable time with our families. Yes, James is writing to those of us who are under pressure.

Happy (blessed) is the person who perseveres under trial, who stands his ground. Why is he happy? Because after the test, he will receive the "crown of life." (James 1:12) In the ancient Grecian games a wreath was placed on the victor's head as a sign of honor and victory. This "crown" (*stephanos*) is what Paul had in mind when he wrote his last letter to Timothy from a prison cell in Rome: "I fought the good fight, I've finished my race, I have kept the faith. Henceforth, there is laid up for me a crown of righteousness, which the Lord, the righteous judge, will give to me in that day and not to me only but to all those who love his appearing" (II Tim. 4:7–8). The man or woman who stands firm will receive this crown of life. God has a special reward for patient sufferers. In the end, stress is certainly profitable.

As a pastor I've watched many men and women face special circumstances and difficulties and even death. Not long ago I went through the traumatic experience of watching one of my best friends die a long and agonizing death. I watched him die as he had lived, persevering under trial. Never once did I hear him complain. During our last visit, I read him the promises of God concerning the great marriage supper of the Lamb and the crown of life which the Lord, the righteous judge, will give us on that day. As I left the hospital room and looked back for a parting smile, his final words to me were, "I'll save you a place at the table."

Echoing the theme of James 1:12, the Apostle John wrote these inspired words from God: "Do not fear any of those things which you are about to suffer. Indeed, the devil is about to throw some of you into prison, that you may be tested and you will have tribulation ten days. Be faithful unto death and I will give you the crown of life" (Rev. 2:10). No wonder Fanny Crosby, who endured the stress of blindness for a lifetime said:

> *Great things he has taught us,*
> *great things he has done,*
> *And great our rejoicing through Jesus the Son;*
> *But purer and higher and greater will be*
> *Our wonder, our transport, when Jesus we see.*

Stress…it is the menace of modern man and of modern ministers. How do we handle it? Remember it is predictable. It is a question of *when*, not *if*. It is not going to go away. Not one of us is immune. Stress is also problematic. If we do not deal with it, stress it can be destructive. Stress is also paradoxical. We can count it as joy because we know that the final eternal outcome will be glorious. Stress is also purposeful. God is testing us, putting us through the furnace so that we might come forth as gold. Finally, stress is profitable. Think ahead to the crown of life!

The very word "victory" implies a struggle. Consider the struggle of a butterfly to emerge from its cocoon. Once there was a little boy who found a cocoon attached to a small branch of a tree. He took the branch home and kept it securely in his room. When spring came, the butterfly began to struggle to escape from its prison. Wanting to help, the boy found a pair of small scissors and made a slight incision in the cocoon. Soon the butterfly emerged in all of its radiant beauty. But it never flew! Having escaped all the struggles to emerge from the cocoon, the muscles of its wings never developed. The boy's good intentions robbed the butterfly of its power to soar. Yes, perseverance must finish its work so that we may be mature and complete, not lacking anything.

When we study the Gospels we quickly discover that no one was ever confronted with more stressful situations than our Lord Jesus Christ. He knew the stress of knowing that His own family in Nazareth thought He was mentally disturbed and had practically lost His mind. He spent over three years training His own ministerial and management team. He knew the stress of seeing one of them become a traitor. He knew the stress of watching the rest of them as they would not stand with Him when the chips were really down. He knew the stress of being falsely charged, beaten, mocked, and finally cruelly executed. Talk about high anxiety in the highest calling anyone ever had! And yet, as always, our Lord is our model in learning to deal with stress.

The Lord Jesus dealt with stress by being fit physically. He knew the physical pressures of the crowd pressing in upon Him constantly. Jesus did not get up in the morning and get on the treadmill. He didn't have to do so. Why? He did not get in the car and drive to the office, drive to visit the hospitals, or drive to His appointments. He walked! In the Gospels we find Him on one occasion walking over 100 miles in three days and once he walked from Sidon to Tyre, a distance of almost 50 miles in one day. He must have been in very good cardiorespiratory condition. His was a physically active lifestyle. He spent His first 30 years as a carpenter. In his day there was no lumber yard to purchase his supplies. He had to harvest timber himself from the forest, haul it back to the shop, and then prepare it into lumber. There were no electric saws or power tools. It was hard physical work. Jesus dealt with stress by leading a very active physical lifestyle. And He knew the importance of rest as well. How often do we find Him going up into some mountain alone or finding refuge and rest in the home of the likes of Mary and Martha and Lazarus?

Today, so many of our ministers do not deal with stress in the physical realm. When we really think about it most of our church work is taken up with sitting. We go to

church and we sit, we go to Bible study and we sit, we go
to mission meetings and we sit, we go into our study and
we sit, we counsel our parishioners and we sit, we go to
committee and deacon meetings and we sit, we go to choir
practice and we sit, and then we get home from a day of
sitting and sit again in front of the television set. When
Jesus truly becomes our champion and Lord we will find
ourselves taking seriously His admonition that our bodies
are His temple and we will take care of our stress in the
physical realm.

Jesus not only knew about physical stress, but He also
knew a great deal about mental stress. This is why He often
got away. He escaped the hustle and bustle of His world
to be alone, to gather His thoughts, to find margin in life.
In Luke's Gospel it says that Jesus often removed himself
from the disciples to be alone (Luke 5:16). Sometimes, we
too need to walk away from the pressures long enough to
get our own thinking straight, to find some margin in our
own lives.

Not only did He experience the stress that comes upon
us physically and mentally but Jesus also knew the spiritual stress that comes with a high calling. All through the
Gospels we find Him giving priority to prayer. In fact, the
busier His life became, the more stressful the circumstances became around Him, the more time He spent in

prayer. He prayed before the stressful situations of life. He prayed during them. And He prayed after them. In Gethsemane we hear Him praying, "My soul is exceedingly sorrowful; deeply grieved." Here is the real battlefield for stress; it is played out of on the battlefield of prayer. James admonishes us across the centuries that, "If any of us lack wisdom let us ask of God" (James 1:5).

In order for stress to become profitable there is something for the minister to do. To begin with he needs to take responsibility in the physical realm. It is time for those in ministry to make a serious commitment to a systematic exercise program and to get serious about a responsible diet. There is also a responsibility in the mental and emotional realm. We need each other. Everyone needs a support network. Life is about relationships and if Jesus saw the need to find respite with three of His friends and to be open enough to share His heart and thoughts with them, how much more do we? And yes, there is responsibility to be taken in the spiritual realm. We need to remember that it is "daily" bread upon which we are to feed. The apostles were instructed to tarry in the upper room until they were "endued" with power from on high (Luke 24:49). Interestingly, we find this Greek verb, *enduo*, in the middle voice which indicates that the subject acts upon him or herself. Thus, they tarried until they "endued themselves" with power. They took responsibility of their own spiritual needs and got right with God and each other.

It should be also noted that there is something for the church to do in helping to relieve the stress of the ministry. To begin with, the church should remember that the "laborer is worthy of his hire." The Apostle Paul often addressed this issue in his epistles. To the Corinthians he wrote that "the Lord commands that those who preach the gospel should be supported by those who receive the gospel" (I Cor. 9:14). To the Galatians he said, "Those who are taught the word must share all good things with their teacher" (Gal. 6:6). And, to his young preacher friend, Timothy, he reminded the church that "the elders who rule well should be counted worthy of double honor, especially those who labor in the Word and in doctrine" (I Tim. 5:17). The church can go a long way in helping to relieve the stressful condition of its ministers by providing adequate salary and benefits. Many churches simply provide their pastor and staff with a "salary package". They do not separate the benefit section from the salary section and thus compensate their minister with a lump sum and ask him to divide it as he likes. Arrangements such as this usually cause the minister to have to pay more taxes than may be legally owed. This results in less money to provide for his family. (For example, by wisely using the "salary and benefit approach" rather than the "package approach", a church can use tax savings on a $40,000 total package effectively to increase the minister's cash salary, net of taxes, by $2,100.) Perhaps the biggest issue today is in the area of medical insurance. Every church, which possibly can, should provide this benefit separate and apart from the minister's salary. A lot of ministerial stress would be diminished with this positive act. Paul reminds us that we have an obligation to provide "especially for those of our own household" (I Tim. 5:8). The Annuity Board has provided a *Planning Financial Support* workbook to help churches in this vital area. It can be obtained by simply calling toll-free 1-800-262-0511.

The church should also encourage the minister to take time away in order to recharge his physical and spiritual batteries. The church should also take more seriously the call to do the work of the ministry herself. The very office of the deacon was born out of a problem in the church. There was a division in the fellowship erupting because the Hellenistic Jews in the early church felt the apostles were showing favoritism to the Hebraic Jewish believers. So wisely, the leaders appointed seven deacons, all of whom had Hellenistic names, to perform the works of the ministry for the church. The result was that the pastors then could devote themselves to "prayer and the ministry of the word."

In the midst of all the high anxiety that comes with our high calling may we, like our spiritual forefathers before us, "cast all our cares and anxieties on Him because He cares for us" (I Pet. 5:7). While stress may be predictable, problematic, paradoxical, and purposeful, it can ultimately be profitable for "blessed is the man who perseveres under stressful trials for he shall receive the crown of life."

Appendices

Appendix A

Well-being means a healthy, balanced life

Appendix B

Getting into shape — safely

Appendix C

A peek at the pyramid: A guide to healthy eating

Appendix D

Become a life-long partner with the Annuity Board

For additional information, visit these helpful wellness Web sites:

www.absbc.org

www.cooperaerobics.com

www.lifeway.com/lwc

Appendix A

Well-being means a healthy, balanced life

In society today, the word healthy means 'absence of disease', but wellness advocates are promoting health as multidimensional and encompassing all parts of our lives.

Each person must take responsibility for his or her own health and well-being. Here are 10 steps to begin the journey to well-being:

1. Well-being begins as a spiritual matter. Life is a gift. We should thank God that we are alive to enjoy it every moment.

2. Each of us is primarily responsible for our own wellness. We have a personal choice in how we react and change with every experience of life.

   Many illnesses could be prevented by living a healthy lifestyle. We can make wise choices to prevent illness and aid in the recovery from disease.

3. Our body, mind and spirit work together. None of these parts can be separated. There is a constant interaction between all three. We must strike a balance where body, mind and spirit work together for the good of the whole.

4. Physical activity is an important factor in maintaining our well-being. Researchers have documented volumes of evidence regarding the health benefits of moderate exercise. People who find the right exercise routines and stay with them consistently find the activity pleasurable and necessary to maintaining a vibrant life.

5. Nutrition is the source of our energy. Smaller, frequent meals with high-quality foods that are low in fat can lead to a healthier life. Since our bodies are mostly water, drinking eight to 10 glasses of water a day is crucial to good health and well-being.

6. Less is best. God created the body to heal itself, but sometimes we need a little help. The doctor who treats what is medically necessary with minimal side effects is a person who truly understands our bodies. The body needs time to heal.

7. How we respond to an event is more important than what happened. Stress is natural and a fact of life.

While we can't change many events, we can change our attitudes and responses which will alter the outcomes.

8. Every moment is precious. Procrastination and worry over what might be robs us of the joy in the present. Of course we should plan for the future, but don't put life on hold for what could happen. Start living now.

9. Creativity is the window to the soul. People with big dreams are people who let themselves dream big. Each of us holds visions in our minds, but never take action to make those dreams come true. Within each of us lies the ability to be creative. Like exercising our muscles, it promotes well-being.

10. God created us, but He isn't finished. Most of our motivation stems from what we perceive as our deficiencies. We are motivated by what we don't have. We want more knowledge so we read more. We want more money so we work more. However, God created us with everything we need to be happy. He created us as complete human beings and gave His Son so that His work might be finished within us. He made us free to grow and develop through giving, serving and loving others. Herein lies the basis for our motivation. Following God gives purpose to our lives. Well-being results from the fulfillment we experience when we are committed to His purpose.

Reference: Focus on Well-Being, Aug. 1998, Vol. 1 Issue 1.

Appendix B

Getting into shape — safely

By Kenneth H. Cooper, M.D., M.P.H.

Before starting a conditioning program, several questions need to be answered. For safety's sake, the level of physical activity you choose needs to suit your age, weight, gender, and medical history. For example, men over age 40 or women over 50 who have not been exercising regularly are strongly urged to get clearance from a physician. It is advisable to have a stress electrocardiogram at that age, even if there's no indication of health problems. If a medical problem such as heart disease or high blood pressure is known or if there's a family history of heart disease, a physical exam is recommended for men at age 35 and women over 40.

Go slowly

Whatever your age, go slowly. Don't expect to get back into condition in 20 days if it took you 20 years to gradually slip out of shape. Building an exercise program slowly, say over 12 to 16 weeks, is much safer and ultimately more effective since you are less likely to get knocked completely off the new program by an injury or strain. In essence, crawl before you walk, and walk before you run.

Warm up

Proper warm-up is another safety measure. Spend three to five minutes stretching and limbering up before you exercise. The older you are, the more likely that your muscles will be tight; to avoid injuring a hamstring or Achilles tendon by moving immediately into the stretch, do some brisk walking before you stretch. In the gym, you can prepare for heavier lifting by first using very light weights. Walk around briskly before you break into a run.

Cool down

It's equally important to cool down gradually. After you exercise vigorously, spend five minutes walking or moving around slowly until your heart rate is back to normal. It's especially important to cool down before going into a sauna, steam room, or whirlpool.

Target your target rate

Keep an eye on the intensity of your workouts. Once you know your target heart rate you can check your pulse during and after exercise or you may decide to wear an electronic heart rate monitor. The idea is to exert yourself enough to get health benefits, but not push yourself too much. One way to see if you are working out too hard is to take your pulse for 15 seconds after you have cooled down for five minutes and multiply by four. If you're under 40 years of age, that number should be less than 120. For anyone 40 to 50, the number should be less than 110, and if you are over 50, the heart rate should be under 100.

Balance your program

Another goal should be to achieve an age-appropriate balance between aerobic exercise and strength training. As a very general guideline, I recommend 20 to 30 minutes of aerobic activity, such as walking or jogging, at least three to five times a week and a 20 minute weight training session (weight machines, hand held weights, or calisthenics) at least twice a week. As you age, the ratio of aerobic exercise to resistance training should change. In your thirties, 80 percent of your physical activity can be aerobic, 20 percent musculoskeletal conditioning. In your forties, aerobic exercise may drop to 70 percent, with 30 percent strength training. It shifts again in your fifties, to perhaps 60/40 and again in your sixties to about 55/45. As we age, we lose muscle mass so it's no good for a sixty-year old to be able to run three miles in 30 minutes if he can't reach over and pick up a sack of groceries without pulling his back out. Women, especially prone to osteoporosis, can help combat bone deterioration by a regular program of strength training.

Be practical

Choose an aerobic challenge that matches your physical condition as well as your interest. This might be brisk walking, running, swimming or cycling. For strength training, use very light weights until you develop muscle strength. To be sure you are using machines or free weights correctly, it is best to have a supervised workout at a reputable fitness center or work with a personal trainer who can also coach you in an overall program. A well-rounded get-fit program must also include attention to your nutrition and stress management.

Listen to your body. Don't ignore pain, particularly recurrent pain. Never ignore any pain in the chest that occurs with exercise. And, if in doubt about anything, play it safe — consult your doctor.

These basic guidelines can help you develop a safe, effective program — one you can keep up for a lifetime.

Remember, fitness is a journey, not a destination. It's not what you did six months ago that counts — it's what you did yesterday, and what you will do tomorrow.

Used by permission: Kenneth H. Cooper, M.D., M.P.H.

Appendix C

A peek at the pyramid:
A guide to healthy eating

By Patty Kirk R.D.,L.D.

Are you often confused by the many options you have for dieting to lose weight? First of all, the focus for weight loss should be healthy eating not dieting. Often times, diets are followed temporarily to simply drop excess pounds. A healthy eating plan is not a diet, but a way of lifelong eating to ensure weight management and optimal health. So, where should you turn for a guide to help you achieve a healthy eating and weight management plan? Take a peek at the Food Guide Pyramid for direction (see page 112).

At the base of the pyramid, you will see that the foods are plant based. The foods that are located on this lowest level are breads, cereals, rice and pasta. Choose products that are whole grain and whole wheat to boost your fiber intake. Six to 11 servings per day from the grain group are recommended. However, for weight loss, choose six to eight servings. Also, the key to managing calories from this group is to watch your portion sizes. A starch serving is a half-cup of cereal, pasta and rice or one slice of bread. To put this in perspective, one cup of bran flakes, two slices of whole wheat bread and one cup of rice would meet the six servings per day recommendation.

Fruits and vegetables form the next tier on the pyramid. Include at least two servings of fruit per day. Vegetables are a key in any weight management or healthy eating program. They are very low in calories and filled with fiber, vitamins and minerals. You can include as many as you would like daily. Be sure to obtain at least three servings of vegetables each day. Your intake of two fruit and three vegetable servings daily allows you to meet the "5-A-Day" for better health recommendations. When speaking about portions and weight management, be sure to watch your intake of starchy vegetables, like potatoes and corn, because their calorie contents are similar to those foods located in the grain group.

Protein is found in both the meat and dairy group. Protein is very important in your diet, but large amounts are not necessary. Keep lean meat, poultry and fish portions small, between five to six ounces per day, to meet your protein needs. Estimating portion sizes does not have to be difficult. To give you an idea, three ounces of meat is approximately the size of a deck of cards or equal to one-half of a typical restaurant portion. Try to include at least three fish entrees per week. Nonfat milk and milk products are an excellent source of calcium that both men and women need. Include at least two calcium-rich food sources each day. Low-fat dairy items are also excellent sources of calcium. For example, one cup of nonfat milk or yogurt and two ounces of two percent or fat-free cheese can be counted as your milk servings for the day and contribute to your daily calcium needs.

At the top of the pyramid are fats and sweets. Include foods located at the top in moderation. Fat is an important nutrient in the diet, but should be used sparingly. Choose olive or canola oil, nuts, avocados and light tub margarines to meet your fat needs. Sweets are also a fun part of life. When seeking weight loss, as a rule of thumb, limit sweets to 125 calories a day for women and 150 calories each day for men. Many sweets can top out at 500-1000 calories and result in weight gain.

Whenever you hear or read about a revolutionary diet to lose weight, first check the recommendations with the pyramid to see how it stacks up. The popular high protein, high fat, low carbohydrate diets turn the pyramid upside down. This results in a diet that is excessive in fats, saturated fat and cholesterol. In addition, these diets are often lacking in fiber and many other important vitamins, minerals and phytochemicals (plant chemicals) that may help prevent cancer and heart disease.

The bottom line: Let the Food Guide Pyramid guide you in your pursuit of healthy eating and weight management. It can be an easy way to achieve your goals.

Used by permission: Patty Kirk R.D.,L.D.

Food Guide Pyramid
A Guide to Daily Food Choices

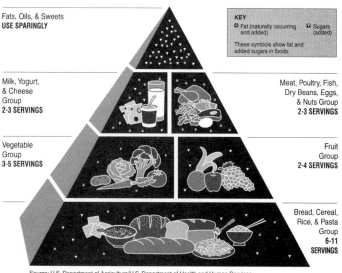

Fats, Oils, & Sweets
USE SPARINGLY

KEY
⬥ Fat (naturally occurring and added)   ⬥ Sugars (added)
These symbols show fat and added sugars in foods.

Milk, Yogurt, & Cheese Group
2-3 SERVINGS

Meat, Poultry, Fish, Dry Beans, Eggs, & Nuts Group
2-3 SERVINGS

Vegetable Group
3-5 SERVINGS

Fruit Group
2-4 SERVINGS

Bread, Cereal, Rice, & Pasta Group
6-11 SERVINGS

Source: U.S. Department of Agriculture/U.S. Department of Health and Human Services

Appendix D

Become a life-long partner with the Annuity Board

If you serve in a Southern Baptist church these para-graphs are unapologetically for you and they could be some of the most important paragraphs you will read. Although you will never "retire" from ministry there will come a day when you will retire from vocational church ser-vice. We want that to be a great day for you. And it can be, if you are prepared.

It is important to get started early in retirement planning. There is a thing called compound interest, which is extremely powerful. For example, assuming an 8% annual return, if a twenty-five year old minister put fifty dollars per month in his retirement account it would be worth $174,550 at age sixty-five. If the same person waited until just the age of thirty-five to begin saving for retirement with the same fifty dollars per month it would be worth $74,520 at age sixty-five, a difference of $100,000. It is very important to start early, but it is also important to start wherever you are along the way to retirement.

The beautiful and beneficial part of being in the Annuity Board program is the protection section. Did you know that if you or your church contribute only a few dollars per month to your retirement, you automatically receive at no cost a survivor's benefit worth up to $100,000 to whomever you designate as your beneficiary? You also receive at no cost a $500 per month disability benefit simply by being a part of the Annuity Board retirement program. This benefit is a cooperative effort provided by your state Baptist convention and the Annuity Board and is a safety net every church should utilize for their ministers.

Just as the Annuity Board helps with your retirement planning, we can also help protect your family's financial security today. Term life and accident plans help provide for your family's day-to-day needs in the event of your or your spouse's illness, injury or death. Our disability plans help protect your income should you become unable to work for a period of time due to injury or illness. Medical coverage is available for times of illness. Dental coverage protects your family's healthy smiles. Whether it's the joy of the birth of a child or the sorrow of serious illness, we want to walk alongside you today and through every season of life.

We at the Annuity Board want to be a life-long partner with you throughout your entire ministry. This is the driving reason behind new products which now give you additional opportunities to save for retirement, or whatever your saving needs. You now have available to you savings vehicles in addition to your regular 403(b) plan that includes Personal Investing Accounts and IRAs (Traditional and Roth IRAs). These opportunities are also available to spouses of persons eligible to participate in Annuity Board plans. Perhaps you have a retirement accumulation in a 401(k) plan from a previous employer. You may want to consider "rolling over" that accumulation into your retirement account or into a rollover IRA.

For more information about these new personal investing products, matching contributions from your state conventions, the protection section at no cost, housing allowance advantages in retirement, our mission church assistance fund, our relief ministries or any of our other services, visit us on the World Wide Web at *www.absbc.org* or better yet, call us at 1-800-262-0511 and speak personally to one of our Customer Relations specialists.